# BILLIE JEAN!

## How Tennis Star Billie Jean King Changed Women's Sports

*by* **MARA ROCKLIFF**

*illustrated by*
**ELIZABETH BADDELEY**

putnam

G. P. PUTNAM'S SONS

Anything Billie Jean did, she did it ALL THE WAY.

When she ran, she ran *fast*.

When she played, she played *hard*.

Billie Jean dreamed of growing up to be just like her hero, Mickey Mantle.

One day, her father took her to a baseball game.

Billie Jean realized something terrible: all of the players on the field were MEN.

What was a girl who loved sports supposed to do?

"How about tennis?" asked her parents. "Girls play tennis."

Billie Jean had never heard of tennis. But if she could run and jump and hit a ball, it sounded good to her.

She saved up her nickels, dimes, and pennies, bought a tennis racket . . .

and went off to a lesson at the public park.
On her very first swing, she hit the ball over the net.

From then on, it was tennis
ALL THE WAY for Billie Jean.

Billie Jean learned fast. Soon, she was ready to play in her first tournament.

On the big day, she wore the nice white tennis shorts her mother had sewn. But when the players gathered for a photo, Mr. Jones, the man in charge, told Billie Jean to stand aside. GIRLS were supposed to wear a dress or skirt.

*"Peanut butter!"* grumbled Billie Jean. She would show them all what really mattered wasn't what she wore, but how she played the game.

Billie Jean practiced more than ever.

She ran *faster*.

She played *harder*.

After three years, she was so good, Mr. Jones agreed to let her go to the national championship—IF she beat the one girl she had never beat before.

When Billie Jean walked out onto the court, the net looked very high. The other girl looked very far away.

Billie Jean bounced the ball twice for luck. Then she tossed it in the air and served.

The match didn't last long. Even Billie Jean was
surprised. Not only had she won, she'd done it in just two sets.
She was going to the nationals—all the way across the country in Ohio!
    But she couldn't go alone, Mr. Jones said. GIRLS had to have a chaperone.
    *Two* airplane tickets? Billie Jean could barely pay for one! She and her mother
had to take the train instead—a three-day ride.

By high school, she was one of the best teenage players in America. But no one paid any attention to girls' sports.

Hardly anybody noticed when Billie Jean left for England two days before graduation. She was going to compete at the most famous, most important tennis tournament in the whole world.

The fans at Wimbledon loved Billie Jean. They leaned forward when she charged up to the net to smash the ball.

They laughed at the way she yelled "Peanut butter!" when she missed a shot.

They applauded when she tossed her racket in the air after she won a match.

Still, back home, no one seemed to care.

At college, even the worst tennis player on the boys' team got a scholarship. Billie Jean could beat the best of them, and yet she had to work two jobs to pay for school.

But Billie Jean kept practicing.

She ran the *fastest*.

She played the *hardest*.

Five years after her first Wimbledon, Billie Jean won.

Being a world tennis champion meant answering
a lot of questions.

But reporters never asked about Billie Jean's game.

The newspapers called Billie Jean a "housewife." In fact, her tennis paid the bills. But women tennis players were paid less than men—much less. And the prizes for the men kept getting bigger, while the prizes for the women shrank.

The men in charge of tennis said it just made sense. After all, fans came to see the men, didn't they? Nobody cared about women's sports.

Peanut butter!

Billie Jean believed fans wanted to see *good* tennis—no matter who was playing. Eight other top players agreed. Together, they started an all-women's tennis tour.

Billie Jean sold tickets . . .

talked to fans . . .

answered questions from
reporters . . .

WHERE'S YOUR HUSBAND?

DOES HE MIND THAT YOU'RE AWAY?

AREN'T YOU READY TO QUIT TENNIS AND HAVE BABIES?

and still played harder than anyone else.

In 1972, Billie Jean won all three of the biggest
tournaments—the French Open, the U.S. Open, and,
of course, Wimbledon. *Sports Illustrated* magazine
named her its first-ever Sportswoman of the Year.
Fans loved Billie Jean—and women's tennis.

Not everyone was happy, though.

Once, Bobby Riggs had been a world tennis champion. He missed those days. When he saw women players getting money and attention, he wanted more money and attention, too.

Bobby told reporters that men were the best at everything, including tennis. He said any man could easily beat any woman. He said he could beat Billie Jean.

The match was called "The Battle of the Sexes," and it was about much more than tennis.

All over the United States, women were fighting for equal rights. But not everyone believed that men and women should be equal.

Billie Jean knew that if she lost to Bobby Riggs, some people would say women couldn't play tennis—or do anything—as well as men. This was a match she *had* to win.

On September 20, 1973, the Houston Astrodome held the biggest, loudest, most excited tennis crowd in history.

Across the country and around the world, millions more watched on TV as famous sportscaster Howard Cosell announced:

"Here comes Billie Jean King . . ."

Howard Cosell said Billie Jean was pretty. He said if she let her hair grow long and took her glasses off, she'd look just like a movie star.
Peanut butter!
Billie Jean wasn't there to look pretty. She was there to WIN.

Billie Jean took her place on the court. She bounced the ball twice.
Then she bounced it twice again and served.

Bobby ran.

But Billie Jean ran faster.

Bobby played hard.

But Billie Jean played harder.

Because anything she did, she did it ALL THE WAY.

When Billie Jean won, she tossed her racket in the air.
The crowd went wild.

Across the country and around the world, girls and women cheered.

Many boys and men cheered, too.

That night, a lot of people changed their minds about what a woman could do.

And children dreamed of growing up
to be just like their hero, Billie Jean.

# AUTHOR'S NOTE

BILLIE JEAN MOFFITT (later King) was born November 22, 1943, in Long Beach, California. When she was five years old, Billie Jean told her mother, "I'm going to do something great with my life." At age eleven, she discovered tennis, and she knew she'd found her goal: to be the greatest tennis player in the world.

At that time, tennis was a game for rich people, and Billie Jean's family wasn't rich. They couldn't afford to join a country club, pay for private lessons, or fly her from tournament to tournament. Billie Jean didn't look like a typical tennis player, either. She wore glasses. She was not slender and graceful. She had breathing problems, and her knees were bad.

Despite all this, Billie Jean King became a tennis superstar. She won thirty-nine Grand Slam championships, including a record twenty at Wimbledon. She was the first woman athlete to earn $100,000 in one year. Not content with success for herself alone, she worked for equal pay for all women in tennis. When a new union of tennis professionals excluded women, she convinced her fellow players to band together in the Women's Tennis Association. In 1973, the U.S. Open offered men and women equal prizes for the first time ever, and much of the credit went to Billie Jean.

Billie Jean fought for opportunities for all women and girls in sports. After she won the Battle of the Sexes, she teamed up with Olympic swimmer Donna de Varona to create the Women's Sports Foundation. At a time when girls' varsity sports got just a penny for every dollar spent on boys, the Women's Sports Foundation pushed for fair treatment under Title IX, a 1972 law against discrimination in publicly funded education. Taking her star power to Washington, Billie Jean testified before the Senate Subcommittee on Education to support girls' sports.

**SELECTED SOURCES**

King, Billie Jean, with Kim Chapin. *Billie Jean*. New York: Harper & Row, 1974.

King, Billie Jean, with Frank Deford. *Billie Jean*. New York: The Viking Press, 1982.

King, Billie Jean, with Christine Brennan. *Pressure Is a Privilege*. New York: LifeTime Media, 2008.

Roberts, Selena. *A Necessary Spectacle: Billie Jean King, Bobby Riggs, and the Tennis Match that Leveled the Game*. New York: Crown, 2005.

Ware, Susan. *Game, Set, Match: Billie Jean King and the Revolution in Women's Sports*. Chapel Hill: The University of North Carolina Press, 2011.

In the 1980s, Billie Jean faced widespread public backlash when a former girlfriend "outed" her as gay. Acknowledging the relationship, she became one of the first openly gay superstar athletes and went on to speak out against discrimination in all forms. She also helped raise money to fight AIDS, joining the rock star Elton John, a friend who wrote his hit song "Philadelphia Freedom" in tribute to Billie Jean's tennis team.

When, in 2007, Wimbledon at last offered equal prizes to women players, winner Serena Williams turned to the stands to thank Billie Jean King. Two years later, Billie Jean was the first woman athlete and the first gay athlete to receive the Presidential Medal of Freedom. Fastening it around her neck, President Barack Obama recalled watching the Battle of the Sexes on TV when he was twelve years old—and rooting for Billie Jean.

*"Every woman ought to be able to pursue whatever career or personal lifestyle she chooses as a full and equal member of society . . . That's a pretty basic and simple statement, but golly, it sure is hard sometimes to get people to accept it."*

*—Billie Jean King, 1974*

*For Alana and Eric: grow up brave, like Billie Jean.—M.R.*

*For my dad, the biggest sports fan I know!—E.B.*

G. P. PUTNAM'S SONS
an imprint of Penguin Random House LLC, New York

Text copyright © 2019 by Mara Rockliff. Illustrations copyright © 2019 by Elizabeth Baddeley.
Penguin supports copyright. Copyright fuels creativity, encourages diverse voices, promotes free speech, and creates a vibrant culture.
Thank you for buying an authorized edition of this book and for complying with copyright laws by not reproducing,
scanning, or distributing any part of it in any form without permission. You are supporting writers and
allowing Penguin to continue to publish books for every reader.

G. P. Putnam's Sons is a registered trademark of Penguin Random House LLC.
Visit us online at penguinrandomhouse.com

Library of Congress Cataloging-in-Publication Data
Names: Rockliff, Mara, author. | Baddeley, Elizabeth, illustrator.
Title: Billie Jean! : how tennis star Billie Jean King changed women's sports / Mara Rockliff; illustrated by Elizabeth Baddeley.
Description: New York, NY: G. P. Putnam's Sons, [2019] | Audience: Ages 4–8. | Includes bibliographic references.
Identifiers: LCCN 2018032410 | ISBN 9780525517795 (hardcover) | ISBN 9780525517801 (epub fxl cpb) | ISBN 9780525517818 (kf8/kindle)
Subjects: LCSH: King, Billie Jean—Juvenile literature. | Tennis players—United States—Biography—Juvenile literature.
| Women tennis players—United States—Biography—Juvenile literature.
Classification: LCC GV994.K56 R64 2019 | DDC 796.342092 [B]—dc23
LC record available at https://lccn.loc.gov/2018032410

Manufactured in China by Hung Hing Printing (Heshan) Co., Ltd.
ISBN 9780525517795
1  3  5  7  9  10  8  6  4  2

Design by Eileen Savage. Text set in Arvo.
The art was done in ink, watercolor, acrylic, and digital media.